Step-by-Step
PROBLEM SOLVING

Grade 7

Thinking Kids®
An imprint of Carson-Dellosa Publishing LLC
Greensboro, North Carolina

Credits

Content Editors: Christine Schwab and Heather Stephan
Copy Editors: Deborah Prato and Julie B. Killian
Layout and Cover Design: Lori Jackson

Visit *carsondellosa.com* for correlations to Common Core, state, national, and Canadian provincial standards.

Copyright © 2012, SAP Group Pte Ltd

Thinking Kids®
An imprint of Carson-Dellosa Publishing LLC
PO Box 35665
Greensboro, NC 27425 USA
www.carsondellosa.com

Printed in the USA • All rights reserved.   ISBN 978-1-609964-82-5

                                                              03-161191151

Introduction

The **Step-by-Step Problem Solving** series focuses on the underlying processes and strategies essential to problem solving. Each book introduces various skill sets and builds on them as the level increases. The six-book series covers the following thinking skills and heuristics:

Thinking Skills:
- ❏ Analyzing Parts and Wholes
- ❏ Comparing
- ❏ Classifying
- ❏ Identifying Patterns and Relationships
- ❏ Deduction
- ❏ Induction
- ❏ Spatial Visualization

Heuristics:
- ❏ Act It Out
- ❏ Draw a Diagram/Model
- ❏ Look for a Pattern
- ❏ Work Backward
- ❏ Make a List/Table
- ❏ Guess and Check
- ❏ Before and After
- ❏ Make Suppositions
- ❏ Use Equations

Students who are keen to develop problem-solving abilities will learn quickly how to:
- ❏ make sense of the problem sum: what am I asked to find?
- ❏ make use of given information: what do I know?
- ❏ think of possible strategies: have I come across similar problems before?
- ❏ choose the correct strategy: apply what I know confidently.
- ❏ solve the problem: work out the steps.
- ❏ check the answer: is the solution logical and reasonable?

Practice questions follow after each skill-set example, and three graded, mixed practices (easy, intermediate, challenging) are provided for an overall assessment of the skills learned. The worked solutions show the application of the strategies used. Students will find this series invaluable in helping them understand and master problem-solving skills.

S. Leong

Table of Contents

Strategy Summary

The following summary provides examples of the various skill sets taught in Step-by-Step Problem Solving.

Page 6 Skill Set 1: Analyzing Parts and Wholes

Analyzing parts and wholes is a basic and useful way of looking at a problem. To analyze parts and wholes is to recognize the parts and understand how they form the whole.

Example: A group of 4 boys and 6 girls sold a total of 680 raffle tickets. Each girl sold 25 more tickets than each boy. How much money did the boys raise if each ticket cost $2?

Think
- Whole: 680 tickets; Part: girls → 25 × 6 more tickets than boys
- Draw the model.
- Solve by calculating the excess based on the model.

Solve

$25 \times 6 = 150$

$680 - 150 = 530$

$10 \text{ units} \rightarrow 530$

$\quad 1 \text{ unit} \rightarrow 530 \div 10 = 53$

$\quad 4 \text{ units} \rightarrow 53 \times 4 = 212$

$212 \times \$2 = \$424$

Answer The boys raised **$424**.

Page 9 Skill Set 2: Comparing

Comparing is an effective way of identifying the relationship between the variables in a problem. Comparing the information in a problem helps you determine the differences in variables' quantities (for example, more or less).

Example: The ratio of the number of boys to the number of girls at the zoo was 5:3. After 120 boys left the zoo, 240 more boys than girls were still at the zoo. How many kids were at the zoo to begin with?

Think
- Draw a model to represent the ratio 5:3.
- Fill in the data: 120 boys left, 240 more boys than girls.
- Compare and solve by using the unitary method based on the model.

Solve

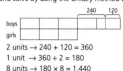

$2 \text{ units} \rightarrow 240 + 120 = 360$

$1 \text{ unit} \rightarrow 360 \div 2 = 180$

$8 \text{ units} \rightarrow 180 \times 8 = 1,440$

Answer 1,440 kids were at the zoo to begin with.

Page 12 Skill Set 3: Identifying Patterns and Relationships

In number and pattern sequences, a relationship often exists among the data in the given arrangement. Always look for specific variations between two or more attributes in the relationship that form a reliable or repeated pattern.

Example: Raul writes his name in the following way:

R A U L L U A R R A U L L U A R . . . ?

1st   99th

Which letter is in the 99th position?

Think
- Look for a pattern.
- RAULLUAR is repeated as a group of 8 letters.
- Solve by using multiples of 8.

Solve

$99 \div 8 = 12 \text{ R}3$

12 groups of 8 → 96 letters

R   A   U   L   L   U   A   R

                           97th 98th 99th

Answer The letter in the 99th position is **U**.

Page 15 Skill Set 4: Deduction

Deduction is a higher-order thinking skill that requires you to infer repeated computations from a given generalization. The information derived from the generalization will lead to a specific answer.

Example: Three friends, Kelly, Shannon, and Tasha, join a volleyball team. They play as a setter, a middle blocker, and an outside hitter. Of the three girls, one is in grade 6, another is in grade 7, and the last is in grade 8. Use the following clues to determine the position and grade level of each girl.

1. Kelly is not the setter.
2. Shannon has been in school longer than the middle blocker.
3. The middle blocker has been in school longer than the outside hitter.
4. Either Shannon is the setter or Kelly is the middle blocker.

Think
- Draw a table to eliminate possibilities using the information given.
- Use logic and reasoning to deduce the answer.

Solve

	Setter	Middle Blocker	Outside Hitter
Grade 6	~~Kelly~~ Shannon	~~Shannon~~	~~Shannon~~ Kelly ✓
Grade 7	~~Kelly~~	~~Shannon~~ Tasha ✓	
Grade 8	~~Kelly~~ Shannon ✓	~~Shannon~~	

Answer **Shannon**, the **setter**, is in **grade 8**. **Tasha**, the **middle blocker**, is in **grade 7**. **Kelly**, the **outside hitter**, is in **grade 6**.

Page 18 Skill Set 5: Induction

Induction is a reverse process of deduction. It is used to draw a general conclusion from specific computations in a problem.

Example: Look at the figures below.

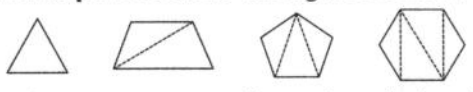

What can you say about the relationship between the number of triangles used to form each figure and the number of sides of the figure? How many triangles are needed to form a figure with *n* sides?

Think

- Gather the information given.
- If necessary, create a table to organize the data.
- Use the data to find a pattern and draw a general conclusion about the relationship.

Solve

Number of Triangles	Number of Sides
1	3
2	4
3	5
4	6

The number of triangles is always 2 fewer than the number of sides.

Answer *n* – 2 triangles are needed to form a figure with *n* sides.

Page 21 Skill Set 6: Spatial Visualization

Spatial visualization is a thinking skill often used in upper primary mathematical problems. It requires you to visualize an object or a situation and then manipulate alternatives, sometimes using a diagram, to solve a problem.

Example: Study the figure below. How many cubes are needed to build it?

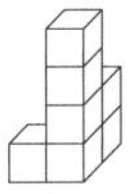

Think

- Visualize the figure from different sides.
- Count the number of cubes by column from the side that gives you the best view.

Solve

From the top view, you will see .
This shows that the figure has 3 columns of cubes.
Counting by column, the figure has 1 + 4 + 2 = 7.

Answer 7 cubes are needed to build the figure.

Page 24 Skill Set 7: Work Backward

Working backward is a strategy that uses a problem's final answer to find what the problem begins with. Very often, you can trace back the steps and reverse the operations to find the answer.

Example: In a school library, 40% of the books are science books, 80% of the remaining books are English books, and the remaining 240 books are math books. What is the total number of books in the library?

Think

- In the end: 20% of the remaining books → 240
- Work backward to find the number of remaining books and then the total number of books.

Solve

$$100\% - 80\% = 20\%$$
$$20\% \text{ of remaining books} \rightarrow 240$$
$$100\% \text{ of remaining books} \rightarrow \frac{240}{20} \times 100 = 1{,}200$$
$$100\% - 40\% = 60\%$$
$$60\% \text{ of all books} \rightarrow 1{,}200$$
$$100\% \text{ of all books} \rightarrow \frac{1{,}200}{60} \times 100 = 2{,}000$$

Answer The total number of books in the library is **2,000**.

Page 27 Skill Set 8: Make a List/Table

Making a list or a table of the information given in a problem helps organize the data. This makes it easier to see missing data or recognize patterns.

Example: When flipped in the air, a coin can land on either of heads (H) or tails (T). Make a list of all possible outcomes when three coins are flipped one at a time. List the combinations that give you two heads out of three coins.

Think

- List all of the possible outcomes systematically.
- Count the number of outcomes that satisfy the question.

Solve

Coin 1	Coin 2	Coin 3	
H	H	H	
H	H	T	✓
H	T	H	✓
T	H	H	✓
H	T	T	
T	H	T	
T	T	H	
T	T	T	

Answer HHT, HTH, THH.

Page 30 Skill Set 9: Use Equations

Using equations to represent a problem is a common heuristic used in upper primary and secondary mathematical problems. This is a quick and effective method to help you become familiar with the formulation and application of various equations.

Example: The figure shows a square with a base of 10 centimeters. What is the area of the shaded part if π = 3.14?

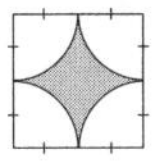

Think

- Figure → 1 square, 4 quarter-circles.
- Use equations for the area of the square and the circle to find the shaded area.

Solve

4 quarter-circles make 1 whole circle.
Because the base of the square is 10 centimeters, the radius of the circle is $\frac{1}{2} \times 10 = 5$ cm.
Area of circle = πr^2 = 3.14 × 5 × 5 = 78.5 cm²
Area of square = length × length = 10 × 10 = 100 cm²
Area of shaded part = 100 cm² − 78.5 cm² = 21.5 cm²

Answer The area of the shaded part is **21.5 square centimeters**.

Page 33 Skill Set 10: Guess and Check

Guess and Check involves making calculated guesses and deriving a solution from them. It is a popular heuristic skill that is often used for upper primary mathematical problems. Because the guesses at the solutions can be checked immediately, the answers are always correct.

Example: Danny has 30 5¢ and 10¢ stamps. The total value of the stamps is $2.40. How many 5¢ stamps does Danny have?

Think

- Data given: 30 stamps → 5¢, 10¢; total value → $2.40.
- Create a guess-and-check table.
- Make at least three guesses to find the answer.

Solve

5¢ Stamps	Value	10¢ Stamps	Value	Total Value	Check
15	$0.75	15	$1.50	$2.25	✗
14	$0.70	16	$1.60	$2.30	✗
12	$0.60	18	$1.80	$2.40	✓

Answer Danny has **12 5¢ stamps**.

Page 36 Skill Set 11: Before and After

This heuristic skill can be used to solve problems with two scenarios. By placing data into before-and-after diagrams or mathematical representations and then making a comparison, you will be able to solve the problems easily.

Example: Carla and Zach had a total of $216. After Carla's mother gave her another $51 and Zach spent $\frac{1}{2}$ of his money, both kids had the same amount of money. How much money did each of them have to begin with?

Think

- Before: Carla + Zach → $216; After: Carla + $51 = $\frac{1}{2}$ × Zach
- Draw before-and-after models based on the information given.
- Solve by using the unitary method.

Solve

3 units → $216 + $51 = $267
1 unit → $267 ÷ 3 = $89
Zach → 2 units → $89 × 2 = $178
Candy → $89 − $51 = $38

Answer Carla had **$38** and Zach had **$178** to begin with.

Page 39 Skill Set 12: Make Suppositions

Making suppositions is another higher-order heuristic skill that is often used for upper primary mathematical problems. The skill requires you to make an assumption about a problem before you attempt to solve it.

Example: Seth has 30 5¢ and 10¢ stamps. If the total value of the stamps is $2.55, how many 5¢ stamps does Seth have?

Think

- Make an assumption that Seth has either all 5¢ stamps or all 10¢ stamps.
- Look for a shortage or an excess in the value of the stamps and solve accordingly.

Solve

Assuming all of Seth's stamps are 10¢ stamps,
30 × 10¢ = $3.00
$3.00 − $2.55 = $0.45 (shortage)
10¢ − 5¢ = 5¢
$0.45 ÷ $0.05 = 9

Answer Seth has **9 5¢ stamps**.

Skill Set 1: Analyzing Parts and Wholes

Analyzing parts and wholes is a basic and useful way of looking at a problem. To analyze parts and wholes is to recognize the parts and understand how they form the whole.

Example:

A group of 4 boys and 6 girls sold a total of 680 raffle tickets. Each girl sold 25 more tickets than each boy. How much money did the boys raise if each ticket cost $2?

 Think

- Whole: 680 tickets; Part: girls → 25 × 6 more tickets than boys
- Draw the model.
- Solve by calculating the excess based on the model.

 Solve

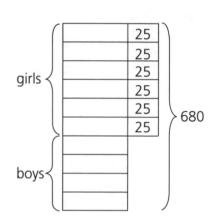

$25 \times 6 = 150$

$680 - 150 = 530$

10 units → 530

1 unit → $530 \div 10 = 53$

4 units → $53 \times 4 = 212$

$212 \times \$2 = \$424$

 Answer The boys raised **$424**.

Give it a try!

A store sold 4 tables and 5 chairs for $752. Each table cost $80 more than each chair. How much did the chairs cost altogether?

 Think

Fill in the data and solve by calculating the excess based on the model.

 Solve

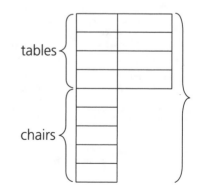

_____ × _____ = _____

_____ − _____ = _____

_____ units → _____

1 unit → _____ ÷ _____ = _____

_____ units → _____ × _____ = _____

 Answer The chairs cost _____.

(Answer: $240)

Practice: Analyzing Parts and Wholes

1. A group of 3 women and 5 men picked 97 pounds of strawberries at their family's farm. Each man picked 5 pounds of strawberries more than each woman. If each pound of strawberries could be sold for $3, how much money would the men make?

💡 **Think**

✏️ **Solve**

⭐ **Answer**

2. Mr. Walsh bought 3 mangoes and 6 melons that weigh 3.6 kilograms altogether. Each melon weighs 300 grams more than each mango. How much do the melons weigh in all?

💡 **Think**

✏️ **Solve**

⭐ **Answer**

3. In a day, 4 cars and 5 taxis travel a total of 125 kilometers. Each taxi travels 7 kilometers more than each car. How much gas do the cars use in a day if they use 1 liter of gas for every 10 kilometers traveled?

💡 **Think**

✏️ **Solve**

⭐ **Answer**

4. Ms. Johnson bought 4 cakes and 7 pizzas for $224. Each cake cost $12 more than each pizza. How much did the pizzas cost?

💡 **Think**

✏️ **Solve**

⭐ **Answer**

Skill Set 2: Comparing

Comparing is an effective way of identifying the relationship between the variables in a problem. Comparing the information in a problem helps you determine the differences in variables' quantities (for example, more or less).

Example:

The ratio of the number of boys to the number of girls at the zoo was 5:3. After 120 boys left the zoo, 240 more boys than girls were still at the zoo. How many kids were at the zoo to begin with?

 Think
- Draw a model to represent the ratio 5:3.
- Fill in the data: 120 boys left, 240 more boys than girls.
- Compare and solve by using the unitary method based on the model.

 Solve

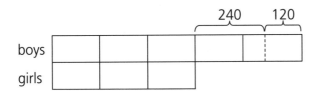

2 units → 240 + 120 = 360

1 unit → 360 ÷ 2 = 180

8 units → 180 × 8 = 1,440

⭐ **Answer 1,440 kids** were at the zoo to begin with.

Give it a try!

A theme park has $\frac{3}{4}$ as many adults as children visiting. If 50 adults and 80 children leave, 100 more children than adults will still be at the theme park. How many people are at the theme park altogether?

 Think
Compare and solve by using the unitary method based on the model.

 Solve

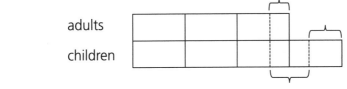

1 unit → _____ − _____ + _____ = _____

_____ units → _____ × _____ = _____

⭐ **Answer** _____ **people** are at the theme park altogether.

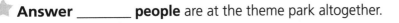
(Answer: 910)

1. The ratio of Monica's weight to Shelby's weight was 9:5. After Monica lost 15 kilograms, she was still 5 kilograms heavier than Shelby. How much did Shelby weigh?

💡 **Think**

✏️ **Solve**

⭐ **Answer**

2. Lisa made an orange drink by mixing orange juice and water at a ratio of 3:8. If she used 400 quarts more water than juice and was still short 50 quarts of water, how much water did Lisa use in all?

💡 **Think**

✏️ **Solve**

⭐ **Answer**

3. The ratio of the area of a triangle to the area of a rectangle is 3:5. The difference in their areas is 54 square inches. What is the height of the triangle if its base is 2 times its height?

💡 **Think**

✏️ **Solve**

⭐ **Answer**

4. Quiana had some beads. The ratio of the number of black beads to the number of white beads was 1:5. After she added 2 more than twice the number of black beads, she still had 18 fewer black beads than white beads. How many black beads and how many white beads did Quiana have to begin with?

💡 **Think**

✏️ **Solve**

⭐ **Answer**

Skill Set 3: Identifying Patterns and Relationships

In number and pattern sequences, a relationship often exists among the data in the given arrangement. Always look for specific variations between two or more attributes in the relationship that form a reliable or repeated pattern.

Example:

Raul writes his name in the following way:

R A U L L U A R R R A U L L L U A R ...?
1st   99th

Which letter is in the 99th position?

 Think

- Look for a pattern.
- RAULLUAR is repeated as a group of 8 letters.
- Solve by using multiples of 8.

 Solve

99 ÷ 8 = 12 R3
12 groups of 8 → 96 letters

R	A	U	L	L	U	A	R
97th	98th	99th					

 Answer The letter in the 99th position is **U**.

Give it a try!

Lin writes her name in the following way:

L I N N I L L L I N N I L L ...?
1st   77th

Which letter is in the 77th position?

 Think

Solve by using multiples of 6.

 Solve

_____ ÷ _____ = _____ R _____

_____ groups of _____ → _____ letters

L   I   N   N   I   L

 Answer The letter in the 77th position is _____.

(Answer: I)

Practice: Identifying Patterns and Relationships

1. Liza creates the following pattern:

L I Z A 1 2 3 L I Z A 1 2 3 . . . ?
1st   88th

Which letter or digit is in the 88th position?

💡 **Think**

✏️ **Solve**

⭐ **Answer**

2. Study the following pattern.

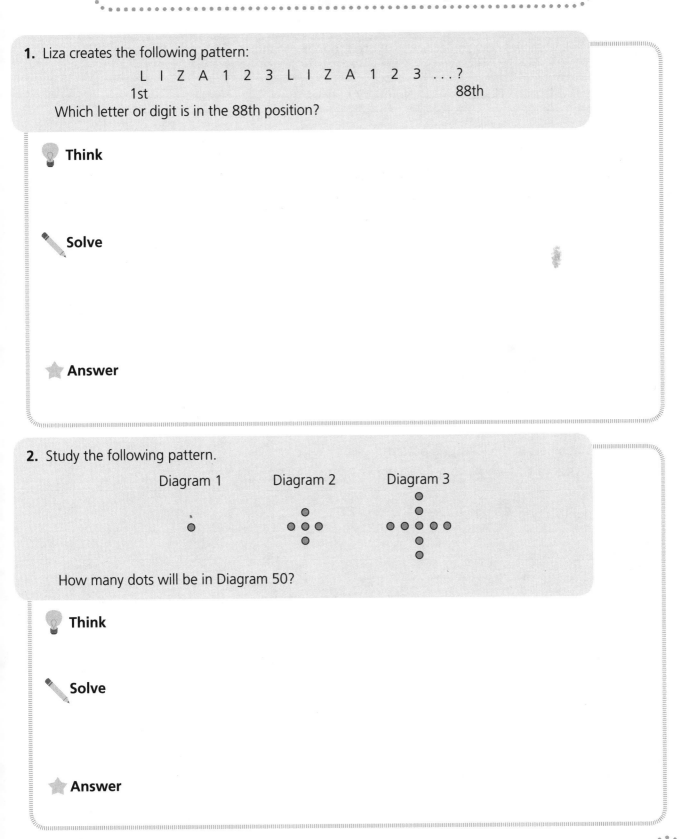

Diagram 1   Diagram 2   Diagram 3

How many dots will be in Diagram 50?

💡 **Think**

✏️ **Solve**

⭐ **Answer**

3. The table below shows how some sticks are used to make triangles. Complete the table.

	Figure	Number of Sticks	Pattern
1	△	3	3
2	△▽	5	3 + 2
3	△▽△	7	3 + 2 × 2
4	△▽△▽		
n			

4. Jan writes numbers in the following pattern:

123454321234321232121123454321234321232121 ...?
1st   999th

Which number is in the 999th position?

 Think

Solve

Answer

Skill Set 4: Deduction

Deduction is a higher-order thinking skill that requires you to infer repeated computations from a given generalization. The information derived from the generalization will lead to a specific answer.

Example:

Three friends, Kelly, Shannon, and Tasha, join a volleyball team. They play as a setter, a middle blocker, and an outside hitter. Of the three girls, one is in grade 6, another is in grade 7, and the last is in grade 8. Use the following clues to determine the position and grade level of each girl.

1. Kelly is not the setter.
2. Shannon has been in school longer than the middle blocker.
3. The middle blocker has been in school longer than the outside hitter.
4. Either Shannon is the setter or Kelly is the middle blocker.

 Think
- Draw a table to eliminate possibilities using the information given.
- Use logic and reasoning to deduce the answer.

 Solve

	Setter	Middle Blocker	Outside Hitter
Grade 6	~~Kelly~~ ~~Shannon~~	~~Shannon~~	~~Shannon~~ Kelly ✓
Grade 7	~~Kelly~~	~~Shannon~~ Tasha ✓	
Grade 8	~~Kelly~~ Shannon ✓	~~Shannon~~	

⭐ **Answer** **Shannon**, the **setter**, is in **grade 8**. **Tasha**, the **middle blocker**, is in **grade 7**. **Kelly**, the **outside hitter**, is in **grade 6**.

Give it a try!

Rashawnda writes the sequence 1 2 4 7 11 16 22 29 37 46 . . .
What is the remainder when the 2,011th number in the sequence is divided by 5?

 Think
Draw a table to deduce the answer.

 Solve

Number	1	2	4	7	11	16	22	29	37	46
Remainder										

The remainders repeat after every _____ numbers.

_____ ÷ _____ = _____ R _____

⭐ **Answer** The remainder is _____.

(Answer: 1)

© SAP Group Pte Ltd • FS-704119

Practice: Deduction

1. Paul, Nathan, and Ava like to eat different types of burgers. The three kids are ages 7, 8, and 9. Deduce their respective ages and favorite burgers by using the following clues :
  1. The 8-year-old does not like veggie burgers.
  2. Nathan is older than Ava, who likes turkey burgers.
  3. Paul, who likes spicy burgers, is older than Ava.

💡 **Think**

✏️ **Solve**

⭐ **Answer**

2. A school has 100 students in grade 6. Of those students, 25 are on the math team, and 40 of them are on the science team. Also, 10% of the students are on both teams. How many students are not on either team?

💡 **Think**

✏️ **Solve**

⭐ **Answer**

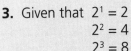

3. Given that $2^1 = 2$

$\qquad 2^2 = 4$

$\qquad 2^3 = 8$

$\qquad 2^4 = 16$

$\qquad 2^5 = 32$

$\qquad 2^6 = 64$

What is the last digit of 2^{100}?

 Think

 Solve

 Answer

4. Someone spilled milk. Mom asked her four daughters, Jenna, Mandy, Nellie, and Sarah, which of them was responsible. The girls answered as follows:

$\qquad$ Jenna: "It wasn't me!"

$\qquad$ Sarah: "It was Nellie!"

$\qquad$ Mandy: "It was Sarah!"

$\qquad$ Nellie: "Sarah is lying!"

If only one of the girls was telling the truth, who spilled the milk?

 Think

 Solve

 Answer

Skill Set 5: Induction

Induction is a reverse process of deduction. It is used to draw a general conclusion from specific computations in a problem.

Example:

Look at the figures below.

What can you say about the relationship between the number of triangles used to form each figure and the number of sides of the figure? How many triangles are needed to form a figure with *n* sides?

 Think

- Gather the information given.
- If necessary, create a table to organize the data.
- Use the data to find a pattern and draw a general conclusion about the relationship.

 Solve

Number of Triangles	Number of Sides
1	3
2	4
3	5
4	6

The number of triangles is always 2 fewer than the number of sides.

 Answer *n* – **2 triangles** are needed to form a figure with *n* sides.

Give it a try!

Look at the figures below.

What can you say about the relationship between the number of sides on each figure and the number of dots on each figure? How many dots would be on a figure with *n* sides?

 Think

Use the data in a table to find a pattern and draw a general conclusion about the relationship.

 Solve

Number of Sides	Number of Dots

 Answer _____ **dots** would be on a figure with *n* sides.

(Answer: 2*n*)

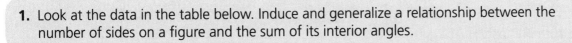

1. Look at the data in the table below. Induce and generalize a relationship between the number of sides on a figure and the sum of its interior angles.

 Think

Number of Sides	Sum of Interior Angles
3	180°
4	360°
5	540°
6	720°

 Solve

 Answer

2. Study the following pattern.

```
            1                    ← line 1
         2   4
       3   6   9
     4   8   12   16
   5   10   15   20   25         ← line 5
```

What can you say about the numbers found in line 18?

 Think

 Solve

 Answer

3. Given 1, 3, 8, 15, . . .
What is the 10th number?

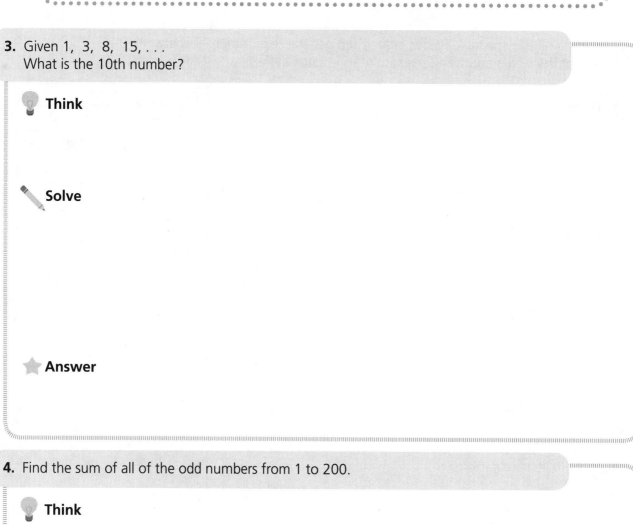

💡 **Think**

✏️ **Solve**

⭐ **Answer**

4. Find the sum of all of the odd numbers from 1 to 200.

💡 **Think**

✏️ **Solve**

⭐ **Answer**

Skill Set 6: Spatial Visualization

Spatial visualization is a thinking skill often used in upper primary mathematical problems. It requires you to visualize an object or a situation and then manipulate alternatives, sometimes using a diagram, to solve a problem.

Example:
Study the figure below. How many cubes are needed to build it?

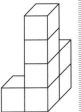

 Think
- Visualize the figure from different sides.
- Count the number of cubes by column from the side that gives you the best view.

 Solve

From the top view, you will see ⬚ .

This shows that the figure has 3 columns of cubes.

Counting by column, the figure has 1 + 4 + 2 = 7.

⭐ **Answer 7 cubes** are needed to build the figure.

Give it a try!

How many cubes are needed to build the following figure if it is empty inside and the walls are only 1 cube thick?

 Think
Visualize the figure as hollow or empty inside.

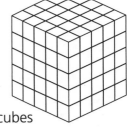

Solve

Volume of solid figure = _____ × _____ × _____ = _____ cubes

Volume of hollow figure = _____ × _____ × _____ = _____ cubes

_____ − _____ = _____

⭐ **Answer** _____ **cubes** are needed to build the figure.

(Answer: 98)

Practice: Spatial Visualization

1. The net of a cube is shown below. What shape or letter is on the top face of the cube?

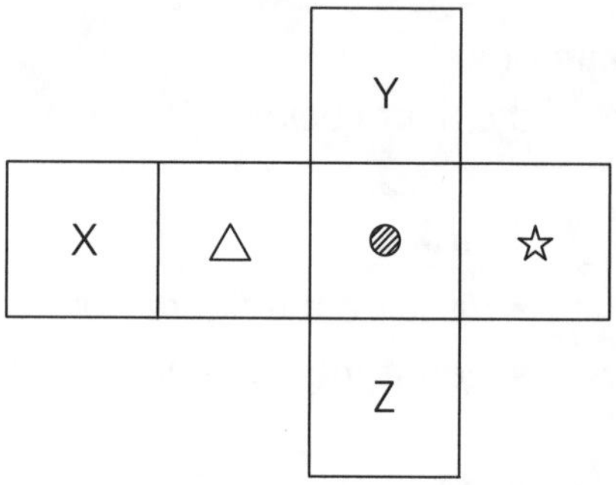

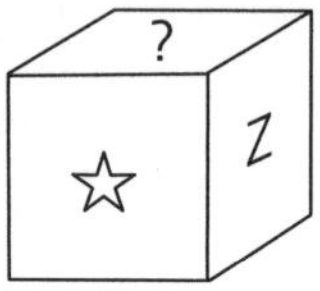

💡 **Think**

✏️ **Solve**

⭐ **Answer**

2. The net of a solid is shown below. Draw how the solid looks when its net is folded up.

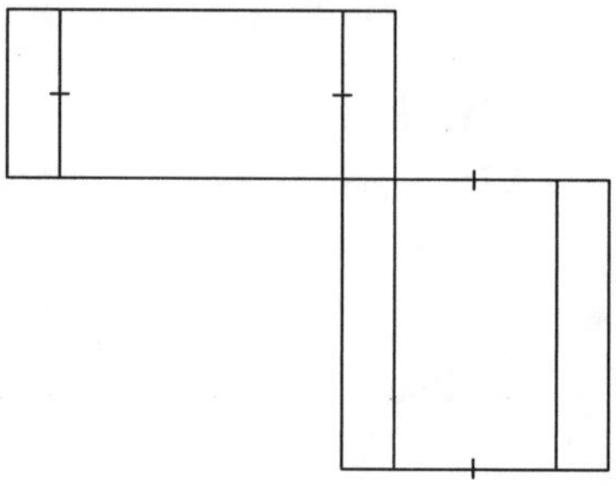

💡 **Think**

✏️ **Solve**

⭐ **Answer**

3. The figure below is a prism. Draw the net of the prism.

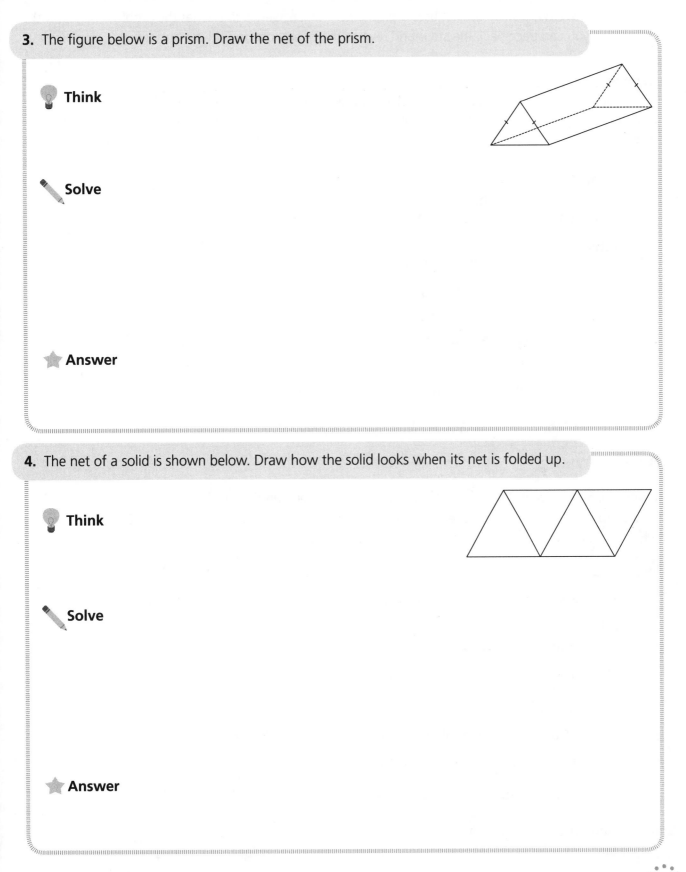

💡 **Think**

✏️ **Solve**

⭐ **Answer**

4. The net of a solid is shown below. Draw how the solid looks when its net is folded up.

💡 **Think**

✏️ **Solve**

⭐ **Answer**

Skill Set 7: Work Backward

Working backward is a strategy that uses a problem's final answer to find what the problem begins with. Very often, you can trace back the steps and reverse the operations to find the answer.

Example:

In a school library, 40% of the books are science books, 80% of the remaining books are English books, and the remaining 240 books are math books. What is the total number of books in the library?

 Think

- In the end: 20% of the remaining books → 240
- Work backward to find the number of remaining books and then the total number of books.

 Solve

$$100\% - 80\% = 20\%$$

20% of remaining books → 240

100% of remaining books → $\frac{240}{20} \times 100 = 1,200$

$$100\% - 40\% = 60\%$$

60% of all books → 1,200

100% of all books → $\frac{1,200}{60} \times 100 = 2,000$

⭐ **Answer** The total number of books in the library is **2,000**.

Give it a try!

In January, Shane spent 30% of his salary on a new cell phone and used 40% of the balance to take a trip. He then saved $\frac{1}{3}$ of his remaining salary, which amounted to $252. What was Shane's monthly salary?

 Think

Work backward to find Shane's remaining salary and then his full monthly salary.

 Solve

remaining salary → $_____ × _____ = $_____

100% − _____% = _____%

_____% of balance salary = $_____

100% of balance salary = (_____ ÷ _____) × 100 = $_____

_____% of full monthly salary → $_____

100% of full monthly salary → (_____ ÷ _____) × 100 = $_____

⭐ **Answer** Shane's monthly salary was _____.

Practice: Work Backward

1. Porchia had some marbles in box A and box B. She moved 25 marbles from box A to box B. She then moved 40 marbles from box B back to box A. In the end, 150 marbles were left in box A, which was twice the number of marbles in box B. How many marbles were in each box to begin with?

💡 **Think**

✏️ **Solve**

⭐ **Answer**

2. Maria had 240 colored tiles in bag X and bag Y. She moved $\frac{3}{5}$ of the tiles from bag X to bag Y. She then moved $\frac{1}{2}$ of the tiles from bag Y back to bag X. In the end, she had twice as many tiles in bag X as she had in bag Y. How many tiles were in each bag to begin with?

💡 **Think**

✏️ **Solve**

⭐ **Answer**

3. Tony and Perry picked strawberries at a farm. Tony gave $\frac{1}{3}$ of his strawberries to Perry. Perry then gathered all of the strawberries he had and gave 25% of them to Tony. Tony counted all of his strawberries and gave $\frac{1}{5}$ of them back to Perry. In the end, Tony had 32 strawberries, and Perry had 56 strawberries. How many strawberries did each of them pick to begin with?

 Think

Solve

 Answer

4. Andre and Byron each had a trading card collection. Andre gave $\frac{3}{4}$ of his cards to Byron. Byron then gave 80% of his cards back to Andre. In the end, Andre had 297 cards, and Byron had 63 cards. How many trading cards did each boy have to begin with?

 Think

Solve

 Answer

Making a list or a table of the information given in a problem helps organize the data. This makes it easier to see missing data or recognize patterns.

Example:

When flipped in the air, a coin can land on either heads (H) or tails (T). Make a list of all possible outcomes when three coins are flipped one at a time. List the combinations that give you two heads out of three coins.

 Think

- List all of the possible outcomes systematically.
- Count the number of outcomes that satisfy the question.

 Solve

Coin 1	Coin 2	Coin 3	
H	H	H	
H	H	T	✓
H	T	H	✓
T	H	H	✓
H	T	T	
T	H	T	
T	T	H	
T	T	T	

⭐ **Answer HHT, HTH, THH.**

Give it a try!

A water tank is filled to its capacity of 132 gallons. Water is then drained from the tank through tap A and tap B at the rates of 18 gallons per minute and 20 gallons per minute, respectively. If tap B is turned on 1 minute after tap A, how long will it take to empty the tank?

 Think

Make a table of the given information and input the data accordingly.

 Solve

	0 min.	1 min.					
Tap A	0	18					
Tap B	0	0					
Total	0	18					

⭐ **Answer** It will take _____ **minutes** to empty the tank.

(Answer: 4)

Practice: Make a List/Table

1. Destini has a 5¢, a 10¢, and a 50¢ stamp. Make a list to show the postage amounts she could have by using one or more stamps. How many different postage amounts could Destini have?

💡 **Think**

✏️ **Solve**

⭐ **Answer**

2. Oil is flowing into tanks X and Y at the rates of 25 gallons per minute and 35 gallons per minute, respectively. However, the tap for tank Y is turned on 2 minutes after the tap for tank X is turned on. How long does it take for tank Y to be filled with as much oil as tank X?

💡 **Think**

✏️ **Solve**

⭐ **Answer**

3. Two dice are thrown. How many combinations could result in even-numbered sums?

💡 **Think**

✏️ **Solve**

⭐ **Answer**

4. Three cars leave town X for town Y at 1-hour intervals. Car A, which leaves first, travels at 50 miles per hour. Car B, which leaves next, travels at 60 miles per hour. Car C, which leaves last, travels at 70 miles per hour. How long does it take car C to catch up with the other cars?

💡 **Think**

✏️ **Solve**

⭐ **Answer**

Skill Set 9: Use Equations

Using equations to represent a problem is a common heuristic used in upper primary and secondary mathematical problems. This is a quick and effective method to help you become familiar with the formulation and application of various equations.

Example:

The figure below shows a square with a base of 10 centimeters. What is the area of the shaded part if $\pi = 3.14$?

 Think

- Figure → 1 square, 4 quarter-circles.
- Use equations for the area of the square and the circle to find the shaded area.

 Solve

4 quarter-circles make 1 whole circle.

Because the base of the square is 10 cm, the radius of the circle is $\frac{1}{2} \times 10 = 5$ cm.

Area of circle = πr^2 = 3.14 × 5 × 5 = 78.5 cm²

Area of square = length × length = 10 × 10 = 100 cm²

Area of shaded part = 100 cm² − 78.5 cm² = 21.5 cm²

 Answer The area of the shaded part is **21.5 square centimeters**.

Give it a try!

The figure below is made up of a circle and a triangle. The area of the circle is 154 square centimeters. What is the area of the shaded part if $\pi = \frac{22}{7}$?

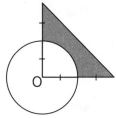

 Think

Use equations for the area of the circle and the triangle to find the area of the shaded part.

 Solve

Area of circle = πr^2 = _____ × _____ × _____ = _____ cm²

So, r = _____ cm

Base of triangle = height of triangle = _____ × 2 = _____ cm

Area of shaded part = area of triangle − $\frac{1}{4}$ × area of circle

= _____ × _____ × _____ − $\frac{1}{4}$ × _____

= _____ − _____

= _____ cm²

 Answer The area of the shaded part is _____ **square centimeters**.

(Answer: $59\frac{1}{2}$)

1. The figure below is made up of a triangle and a rectangle. If 20% of the rectangle is shaded, what is the area of the unshaded part?

 Think

 Solve

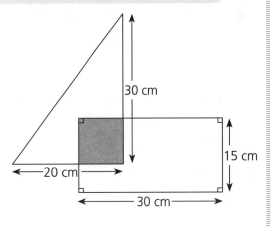

 Answer

---

2. The figure below is formed by two squares, one 6 centimeter and one 4 centimeter. What is the total area of the shaded parts?

 Think

Solve

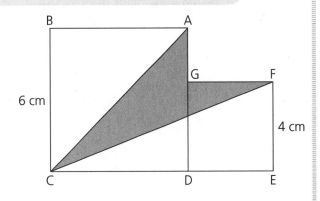

Answer

3. A truck was traveling from Sunshine Town to Lake Town. When it was halfway there, it passed a bus that was traveling in the opposite direction at a constant speed of 56 miles per hour. The truck reached Lake Town $1\frac{1}{4}$ hours later, but the bus was still 30 miles away from Sunshine Town. What was the distance between the two towns?

 Think

 Solve

 Answer

4. Town X and town Y are 780 miles apart. Car A travels from town X to town Y at a speed of 70 miles per hour. Car B travels from town Y to town X at the same time. At what speed is car B traveling if the two cars meet 6 hours later?

 Think

 Solve

 Answer

Skill Set 10: Guess and Check

Guess and Check involves making calculated guesses and deriving a solution from them. It is a popular heuristic skill that is often used for upper primary mathematical problems. Because the guesses at the solutions can be checked immediately, the answers are always correct.

Example:

Danny has 30 5¢ and 10¢ stamps. The total value of the stamps is $2.40. How many 5¢ stamps does Danny have?

 Think

- Data given: 30 stamps → 5¢, 10¢; total value → $2.40.
- Create a guess-and-check table.
- Make at least three guesses to find the answer.

 Solve

5¢ Stamps	Value	10¢ Stamps	Value	Total Value	Check
15	$0.75	15	$1.50	$2.25	✗
14	$0.70	16	$1.60	$2.30	✗
12	$0.60	18	$1.80	$2.40	✓

 Answer Danny has **12 5¢ stamps**.

Give it a try!

Hector has 40 20¢ and 50¢ stamps. The total value of the stamps is $13.70. How many 50¢ stamps does Hector have?

 Think

Make at least three guesses to find the answer.

 Solve

20¢ Stamps	Value	50¢ Stamps	Value	Total Value	Check

Answer Hector has _____ **50¢ stamps**.

(Answer: 19)

Practice: Guess and Check

1. On a particular day, a theater sold a total of 40 adult and child movie tickets. Each adult ticket cost $9, and each child ticket cost $6. If the total value of the tickets sold that day was $294, how many child movie tickets were sold?

💡 **Think**

✏️ **Solve**

⭐ **Answer**

2. A parking lot had 60 vehicles including 2-wheeled motorcycles, 4-wheeled cars, and 6-wheeled trucks. Of those vehicles, 15 were trucks. The vehicles had a total of 250 wheels altogether. How many motorcycles were in the parking lot?

💡 **Think**

✏️ **Solve**

⭐ **Answer**

3. A quiz had 50 questions. The teacher awarded 5 points for every correct answer and deducted 3 points for every incorrect answer. If Ian answered all of the questions on the quiz and scored 98 points, how many questions did he answer correctly?

💡 **Think**

✏️ **Solve**

⭐ **Answer**

4. Libby has 13 $1, $5, and $10 bills in her wallet. If the total amount of money she has is $61, how many of each type of bill does Libby have?

💡 **Think**

✏️ **Solve**

⭐ **Answer**

Skill Set 11: Before and After

This heuristic skill can be used to solve problems with two scenarios. By placing data into before-and-after diagrams or mathematical representations and then making a comparison, you will be able to solve the problems easily.

Example:

Carla and Zach had a total of $216. After Carla's mom gave her another $51 and Zach spent $\frac{1}{2}$ of his money, both kids had the same amount of money. How much money did each of them have to begin with?

 Think

- Before: Carla + Zach → $216; After: Carla + $51 = $\frac{1}{2}$ × Zach
- Draw before-and-after models based on the information given.
- Solve by using the unitary method.

 Solve

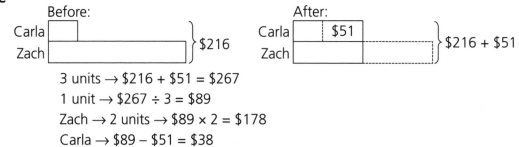

3 units → $216 + $51 = $267

1 unit → $267 ÷ 3 = $89

Zach → 2 units → $89 × 2 = $178

Carla → $89 − $51 = $38

⭐ **Answer** **Carla had $38**, and **Zach had $178** to begin with.

Give it a try!

A club had 352 members. Of those members, 75% were female, and the rest were male. Later in the year, some female members resigned, and the number of female members was then $\frac{3}{7}$ the total number of members in the club. How many female members resigned?

 Think

Solve by using the unitary method.

 Solve

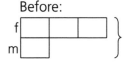

Before: _____ units → _____

    male (1 unit) → _____ ÷ _____ = _____

    female (3 units) → _____ × _____ = _____

After: male (4 units) → _____

    1 unit → _____ ÷ _____ = _____

    female (3 units) → _____ × _____ = _____

    _____ − _____ = _____

⭐ **Answer** _____ **female members** resigned.

(Answer: 198)

Practice: Before and After

1. Wynona is 39 years old. Her son is 5 years old. In how many years will Wynona be 3 times as old as her son?

💡 **Think**

✏️ **Solve**

⭐ **Answer**

2. Mrs. Taylor bought a total of 350 red and green apples. After she sold $\frac{1}{2}$ of the red apples and bought 25 more green apples, she had as many red apples as green apples. How many of each type of apple did Mrs. Taylor buy to begin with?

💡 **Think**

✏️ **Solve**

⭐ **Answer**

3. Lamar kept 415 marbles in tins A, B, C, and D. He took 10 marbles out of tin A and placed 18 more marbles into tin B. He removed $\frac{1}{2}$ of the marbles from tin C and doubled the number of marbles in tin D. After that, each tin had an equal number of marbles. How many marbles were in each tin to begin with?

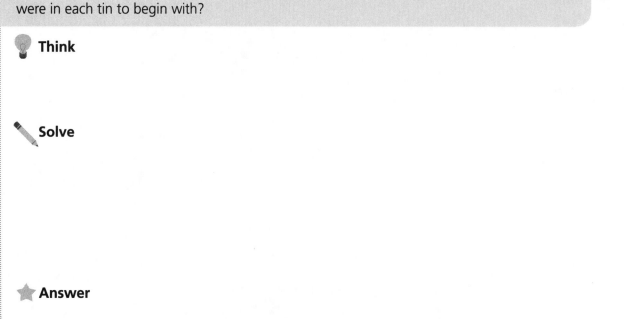

💡 **Think**

✏️ **Solve**

⭐ **Answer**

4. Sabena is 4 years old, and her mother is 36 years old. In how many years will Sabena's mother be 3 times as old as Sabena?

💡 **Think**

✏️ **Solve**

⭐ **Answer**

Skill Set 12: Make Suppositions

Making suppositions is another higher-order heuristic skill that is often used for upper primary mathematical problems. The skill requires you to make an assumption about a problem before you attempt to solve it.

Example:
Seth has 30 5¢ and 10¢ stamps. If the total value of the stamps is $2.55, how many 5¢ stamps does Seth have?

 Think
- Make an assumption that Seth has either all 5¢ stamps or all 10¢ stamps.
- Look for a shortage or an excess in the value of stamps and solve accordingly.

 Solve

Assuming all of Seth's stamps are 10¢ stamps,

$30 \times 10¢ = \$3.00$

$\$3.00 - \$2.55 = \$0.45$ (shortage)

$10¢ - 5¢ = 5¢$

$\$0.45 \div \$0.05 = 9$

⭐ **Answer** Seth has **9 5¢ stamps**.

Give it a try!

A courier company charges $3 for every package delivered safely and pays back $5 for every package lost. If the company was paid $320 for 120 packages, how many packages did the company lose?

 Think
Look for a shortage or an excess in payment and solve accordingly.

 Solve

Assuming all packages were delivered safely,

_____ × _____ = _____

_____ − _____ = _____ (   )

_____ + _____ = _____

_____ ÷ _____ = packages lost

⭐ **Answer** The company lost _____ **packages**.

Practice: Make Suppositions

1. During family day, the Science Center sold a total of 40 adult and child tickets. Each adult ticket cost $8, and each child ticket cost $5. If the total value of the tickets sold that day was $245, how many adult tickets did the Science Center sell?

💡 **Think**

✏️ **Solve**

⭐ **Answer**

2. A parking lot had 55 motorcycles and cars altogether. If the total number of wheels was 194, how many 2-wheeled motorcycles and 4-wheeled cars were in the parking lot?

💡 **Think**

✏️ **Solve**

⭐ **Answer**

3. In a math competition, Yasmin scored 104 points for attempting all 40 questions. If she was awarded 5 points for every correct answer and had 3 points deducted for every incorrect answer, how many questions did Yasmin answer incorrectly?

💡 **Think**

✏️ **Solve**

⭐ **Answer**

4. A store sold 75 skirts and blouses for a total of $960. If each skirt cost $15 and each blouse cost $12, how many skirts and blouses did the store sell?

💡 **Think**

✏️ **Solve**

⭐ **Answer**

Mixed Practice: Easy

1. Mrs. Quan cut a rope into 2 pieces with lengths at a ratio of 3:5. How long was the rope if the longer piece was 40 centimeters longer than the shorter piece?

💡 **Think**

✏️ **Solve**

⭐ **Answer**

2. The total number of marbles in containers A and B is 169. The total number of marbles in containers B and C is 100. The number of marbles in container C is $\frac{2}{5}$ the number of marbles in container A. How many marbles are in container B?

💡 **Think**

✏️ **Solve**

⭐ **Answer**

3. A gallery had 294 ceramic mugs for sale. Xander made $\frac{10}{21}$ of the mugs, and Leo made the rest of the mugs. After some of Xander's mugs were sold, the number of his mugs left was $\frac{4}{15}$ the total number of mugs left. How many of Xander's mugs were sold?

 Think

 Solve

 Answer

4. The net of a solid is shown below. Find the volume of the solid when its net is folded up.

 Think

 Solve

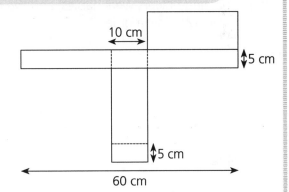

 Answer

5. A car and a van were traveling toward town A. The car passed the van at point X where they were 126 kilometers away from town A. The car arrived at town A $\frac{3}{8}$ of an hour earlier than the van, and the van was still 18 kilometers away. What were the average speeds of the two vehicles?

 Think

Solve

⭐ **Answer**

6. Mr. Garcia ordered some flowers for a party. Of the flowers, 60% were roses, 40% of the remaining flowers were daisies, and the remaining 48 flowers were lilies. How many flowers did Mr. Garcia order?

💡 **Think**

Solve

⭐ **Answer**

7. Square ABCD below is made up of squares of various sizes. If the area of the smallest square is 1 square centimeter, what is the area of square ABCD?

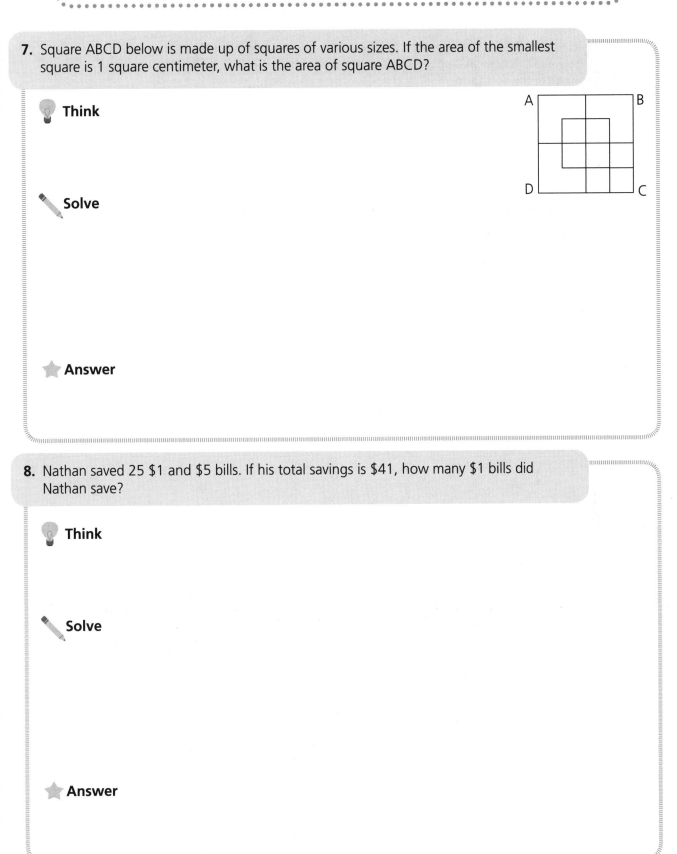

💡 **Think**

✏️ **Solve**

⭐ **Answer**

8. Nathan saved 25 $1 and $5 bills. If his total savings is $41, how many $1 bills did Nathan save?

💡 **Think**

✏️ **Solve**

⭐ **Answer**

9. Edgar walks 480 meters to school every morning at a speed of 48 meters per minute. He walks back from school at a speed of 40 meters per minute. What is Edgar's average walking speed for the round-trip?

 Think

 Solve

⭐ **Answer**

10. Trey took a general knowledge quiz and scored 152 points for attempting 50 questions. If he was awarded 5 points for every correct answer and had 2 points deducted for every incorrect answer, how many questions did Trey answer correctly?

 Think

 Solve

⭐ **Answer**

1. The ratio of the number of ducks to the number of chickens on a farm was 7:4. The farm had 36 more ducks than chickens after 12 ducks ran away. If the farmer bought another 20 ducks and 16 chickens, what percentage of the total number of animals were ducks in the end?

 Think

 Solve

 Answer

2. Study the following pattern. How many dots will be in Figure 34?

Figure 1	Figure 2	Figure 3	. . .	Figure 34
o o	o o o o o o	o o o o o o o o		?

 Think

 Solve

 Answer

3. Below is the net of a special cube. What is the pattern on the top face of the cube?

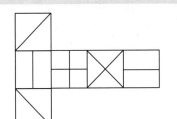

💡 **Think**

✏️ **Solve**

⭐ **Answer**

4. The figure below shows a circle and a right triangle. The center of the circle is N. What is the area of the shaded part if $\pi = \frac{22}{7}$?

💡 **Think**

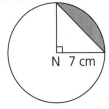

✏️ **Solve**

⭐ **Answer**

5. A bus left town X at 1:00 P.M. and traveled toward town Y. A car left town X for town Y 1 hour later and passed the bus at 3:00 P.M. If the car reached town Y at 3:30 P.M., what time did the bus reach town Y?

💡 **Think**

✏️ **Solve**

⭐ **Answer**

6. A notebook cost $6 and a binder cost $2 more. If Amanda bought a total of 60 notebooks and binders and paid $384 for them, how many notebooks did Amanda buy?

💡 **Think**

✏️ **Solve**

⭐ **Answer**

7. Study the table below. What is *t* in terms of *n*?

Figure	Number	Pattern
1	2	2
2	4	2 + 2
3	6	2 + 2 + 2
⋮	⋮	⋮
n	*t*	

 Think

 Solve

 Answer

8. Class A and class B have a total of 74 students. Class B and class C have a total of 73 students. Class A and class C have a total of 71 students. How many students are in each class?

 Think

 Solve

 Answer

9. Caron and Danielle each had some beads. Caron gave $\frac{1}{3}$ of her beads to Danielle. Danielle then gave $\frac{1}{2}$ of her beads to Caron. Finally, Caron gave $\frac{2}{5}$ of her beads back to Danielle. If Caron had 21 beads and Danielle had 29 beads in the end, how many beads did each of them have to begin with?

 **Think**

 Solve

 Answer

10. Mr. Zucco baked a total of 270 cupcakes and muffins. After he sold $\frac{1}{3}$ of the cupcakes and baked 18 more muffins, he had twice as many cupcakes as muffins. How many cupcakes and muffins did Mr. Zucco bake to begin with?

 **Think**

 Solve

 Answer

1. Given that $3^1 = 3$

$3^2 = 9$

$3^3 = 27$

$3^4 = 81$

$3^5 = 243$

$3^6 = 729$

What is the last digit of 3^{99}?

 **Think**

 **Solve**

⭐ **Answer**

2. Jack and Jaelynn each had some trading cards. Jack gave Jaelynn 8 cards. Jaelynn then gave Jack half of her cards. Finally, Jack gave Jaelynn half of his cards. In the end, Jack had 10 cards and Jaelynn had 30 cards. How many trading cards did each of them have to begin with?

💡 **Think**

✏️ **Solve**

⭐ **Answer**

Mixed Practice: Challenging

3. Ken brought some money on a three-day trip. On day 1, he used half of his money and an additional $100. On day 2, he used half of his remaining money and an additional $50. On day 3, he used half of what he had left and the last $30. How much money did Ken bring on his trip?

💡 **Think**

✏️ **Solve**

⭐ **Answer**

4. The figure below shows a square inside a circle. The radius of the circle is 5 centimeters. What is the area of the shaded region if π = 3.14?

💡 **Think**

✏️ **Solve**

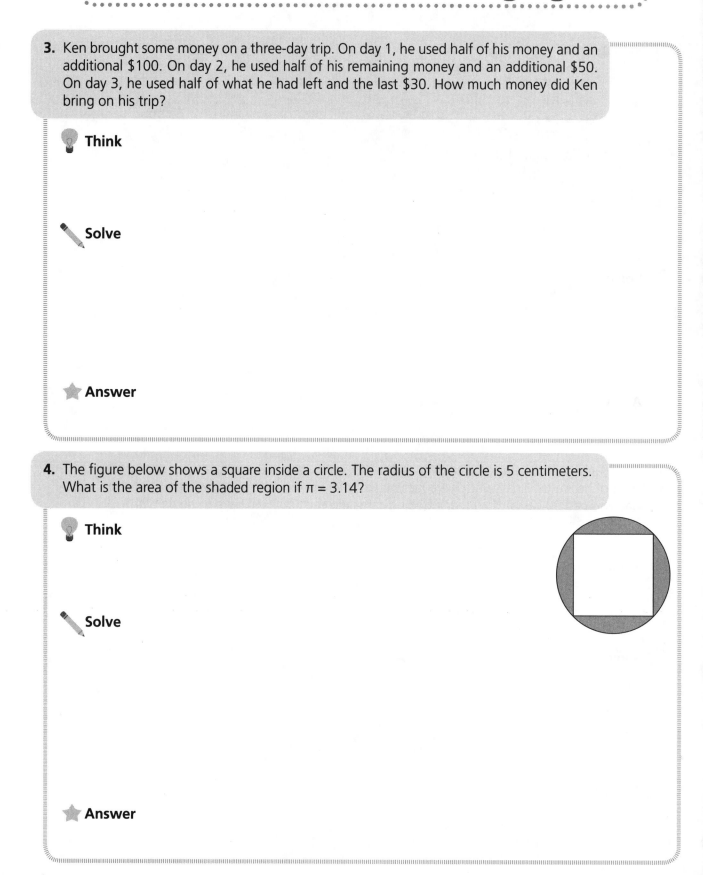

⭐ **Answer**

Mixed Practice: Challenging

5. Erica is 48 years younger than her grandmother. In 4 years, her grandmother will be 4 times as old as Erica. How old is Erica's grandmother?

Think

Solve

Answer

6. A pizza shop made $291 for delivering 15 pizzas. If the shop charged $20 for every pizza delivered on time and offered a 15% discount for every pizza delivered late, how many pizzas did the pizza shop deliver on time?

Think

Solve

Answer

7. Two views of a solid are shown below. How many faces does the solid have?

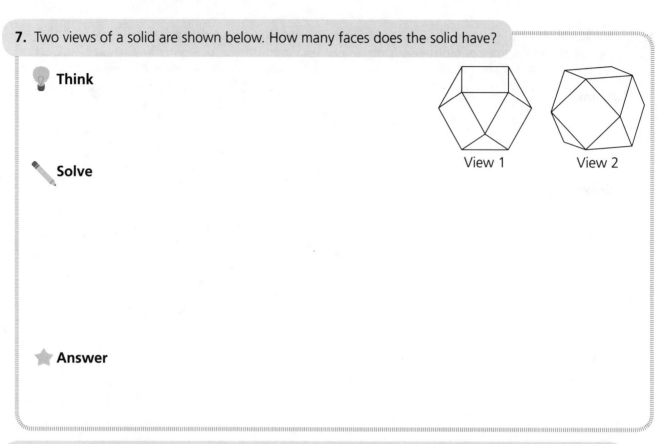

View 1   View 2

💡 **Think**

✏️ **Solve**

⭐ **Answer**

8. The area of the square below is 72 square centimeters. What is the area of the circle if $\pi = \frac{22}{7}$?

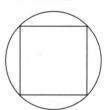

💡 **Think**

✏️ **Solve**

⭐ **Answer**

Answer Key

Analyzing Parts and Wholes

pages 6–8

1.

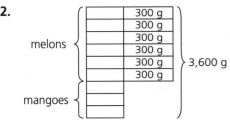

5 lb. × 5 = 25 lb.

97 lb. – 25 lb. = 72 lb.

8 units → 72 lb.

1 unit → 72 kg ÷ 8 = 9 lb.

5 units → 9 kg × 5 = 45 lb.

45 lb. + 25 lb. = 70 lb.

70 × $3 = $210

The men would make **$210**.

2.

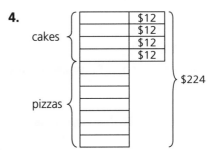

300 g × 6 = 1,800 g

3,600 g – 1,800 g = 1,800 g

9 units → 1,800 g

1 unit → 1,800 g ÷ 9 = 200 g

6 units → 200 g × 6 = 1,200 g

1,200 g + 1,800 g = 3,000 g

The melons weigh **3,000 grams** in all.

3.

7 km × 5 = 35 km

125 km – 35 km = 90 km

9 units → 90 km

1 unit → 90 km ÷ 9 = 10 km

4 units → 10 km × 4 = 40 km

40 ÷ 10 = 4

The cars use **4 liters** of gas in a day.

4.

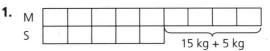

$12 × 4 = $48

$224 – $48 = $176

11 units → $176

1 unit → $176 ÷ 11 = $16

7 units → $16 × 7 = $112

The pizzas cost **$112**.

Comparing

pages 9–11

1.

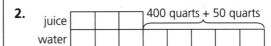

4 units → 20 kg

1 unit → 20 kg ÷ 4 = 5 kg

5 units → 5 kg × 5 = 25 kg

Shelby weighed **25 kilograms**.

2.

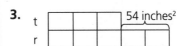

5 units → 450 quarts

1 unit → 450 quarts ÷ 5 = 90 quarts

8 units → 90 quarts × 8 = 720 quarts

Lisa used **720 quarts** of water in all.

3.

2 units → 54 inches²

1 unit → 54 inches² ÷ 2 = 27 inches²

3 units → 27 inches² × 3 = 81 inches²

$$\frac{1}{2} \times base \times height = 81 \text{ inches}^2$$

$$base \times height = 81 \text{ inches}^2 \times 2$$

$$= 162 \text{ inches}^2$$

$$2 \times height \times height = 162 \text{ inches}^2$$

$$height \times height = 81 \text{ inches}^2$$

$$height = 9 \text{ inches}$$

The height of the triangle is **9 inches**.

4.

2 units → 2 + 18 = 20
black → 1 unit → 20 ÷ 2 = 10
white → 5 units → 10 × 5 = 50
Quiana had **10 black beads** and **50 white beads** to begin with.

Identifying Patterns and Relationships
pages 12–14

1. L I Z A 1 2 3 → group of 7 letters and digits
88 ÷ 7 = 12 R 4
4th position → A
The letter in the 88th position is **A**.

2.

Diagram	Number of Dots	Pattern
1	1	1
2	5	1 + 4 × 1
3	9	1 + 4 × 2
4	13	1 + 4 × 3
5	17	1 + 4 × 4
50	197	1 + 4 × 49

197 dots are needed for Diagram 50.

3.

	Figure	Number of Sticks	Pattern
1		3	3
2		5	3 + 2
3		7	3 + 2 × 2
4		9	3 + 2 × 3
n		$2(n-1)+3$	$3+2\times(n-1)$

4. 123454321234321232121 → repeated as a group of 21 numbers.
999 ÷ 21 = 47 R12
12th position → 4
The number in the 999th position is **4**.

Deduction
pages 15–17

1.

Age \ Burger	Veggie	Turkey	Spicy
7		Ava	
8	×		Paul
9	Nathan		

Ava is **7** and likes **turkey burgers**. Paul is **8** and likes **spicy burgers**. Nathan is **9** and likes **veggie burgers**.

2. both teams → $\frac{10}{100} \times 100 = 10$
math only → 25 − 10 = 15
science only → 40 − 10 = 30
not on any team → 100 − 10 − 15 − 30 = 45
45 students are not on either team.

3. The last digits are in the following pattern:
2, 4, 8, 6, 2, 4, ...
    ⏟ groups of 4
100 ÷ 4 = 25 without remainder.
The last digit of 2^{100} is **6**.

4. If Jenna spilled the milk, then she, Sarah, and Mandy would all be lying.
Only Nellie told the truth.
Check:
If Sarah spilled the milk, then only she would be lying. The other three girls all told the truth.
If Mandy spilled the milk, then she and Sarah would be lying. Both Jenna and Nellie told the truth.
If Nellie spilled the milk, then she and Mandy would be lying. Both Jenna and Sarah told the truth.
So, **Jenna** spilled the milk.

Induction
pages 18–20

1. Sum of interior angles is **180° × (number of sides − 2)**.

2. Line 1 → 1 number → multiple of 1
Line 5 → 5 numbers → multiples of 5 (starting from the first multiple)
In line 18, **18 numbers** are **multiples of 18**, starting from the first multiple: 18, 36, 54, 72, . . . , 324.

3. 1st term → 1 = 1
2nd term → 3 = 2^2 − 1
3rd term → 8 = 3^2 − 1
4th term → 15 = 4^2 − 1
For the 10th term, the number is 10^2 − 1 = **99**.

4.

1 + 3 + 5 + 7 + 9 + ⋯ + 191 + 193 + 195 + 197 + 199
50 pairs of 200 = 50 × 200 = 10,000
or
sum of 2 odd numbers → 1 + 3 = 4 = 2 × 2
sum of 3 odd numbers → 1 + 3 + 5 = 9 = 3 × 3
sum of 4 odd numbers → 1 + 3 + 5 + 7 = 16 = 4 × 4
There are 100 odd numbers from 1 to 200.

Sum of 100 odd numbers = 100 × 100
= 10,000
The sum of all odd numbers from 1 to 200 is **10,000**.

Spatial Visualization
pages 21–23

1. The opposite side of Z is Y, so the letter on the top face of the cube is **X**.

2.

3.

4.

Work Backward
pages 24–26

1.

A	B
150	75
− 40	+ 40
110	115
+ 25	− 25
135	90

135 marbles were in box A and **90 marbles were in box B** to begin with.

2. In the end:
3 units → 240
1 unit → 240 ÷ 3 = 80
X → 80 × 2 = 160
Y → 80

X	Y
160	80
− 80	+ 80
80	160

2 units → 80 (left in X after transferring $\frac{3}{5}$ to Y)
1 unit → 40
3 units → 120 (transferred from X to Y)

X	Y
80	160
+ 120	− 120
200	40

200 tiles were in bag X and **40 tiles were in bag Y** to begin with.

3.

	Tony	Perry
End	32	56
Tony gave $\frac{1}{5}$ to Perry	4 units → 32 1 unit → 8 5 units → 40	56 − 8 = 48
Perry gave 25% to Tony	40 − 16 = 24	3 units → 48 1 unit → 16 4 units → 64
Tony gave $\frac{1}{3}$ to Perry	2 units → 24 1 unit → 12 3 units → 36	64 − 12 = 52

Tony picked 36 strawberries and **Perry picked 52 strawberries** to begin with.

4.

	Andre	Byron
End	297	63
Byron gave 80% to Andre	297 − 252 = 45	1 unit → 63 4 units → 252 5 units → 315
Andre gave $\frac{3}{4}$ to Byron	1 unit → 45 3 units → 135 4 units → 180	315 − 135 = 180

Andre and Byron each had **180 trading cards** to begin with.

Make a List/Table
pages 27–29

1. Using 1 stamp: 5¢ 10¢ 50¢
Using 2 stamps: 5¢ + 10¢ = 15¢
5¢ + 50¢ = 55¢
10¢ + 50¢ = 60¢
Using 3 stamps: 5¢ + 10¢ + 50¢ = 65¢
Destini could have **7 different postage amounts**.

2. Make a table:

	0 min.	1 min.	2 min.	3 min.	4 min.	5 min.	6 min.	7 min.
Tank X	0	25	50	75	100	125	150	175
Tank Y	0	0	0	35	70	105	140	175

7 min. − 2 min. = 5 min.
Tank Y takes **5 minutes** to be filled with as much oil as tank X.

3. Make a list.

D1	D2	Sum	D1	D2	Sum
1	1	②	4	1	5
1	2	3	4	2	⑥
1	3	④	4	3	7
1	4	5	4	4	⑧
1	5	⑥	4	5	9
1	6	7	4	6	⑩
2	1	3	5	1	⑥
2	2	④	5	2	7
2	3	5	5	3	⑧
2	4	⑥	5	4	9
2	5	7	5	5	⑩
2	6	⑧	5	6	11
3	1	④	6	1	7
3	2	5	6	2	⑧
3	3	⑥	6	3	9
3	4	7	6	4	⑩
3	5	⑧	6	5	11
3	6	9	6	6	⑫

18 combinations for D1/D2 and
18 combinations for D2/D1.
18 + 18 = 36
There are **36 combinations**.

4.

	1 hr.	2 hr.	3 hr.	4 hr.	5 hr.	6 hr.	7 hr.	8 hr.
Car A	50 mph	100 mph	150 mph	200 mph	250 mph	300 mph	350 mph	400 mph
Car B	0	60 mph	120 mph	180 mph	240 mph	300 mph	360 mph	420 mph
Car C	0	0	70 mph	140 mph	210 mph	280 mph	350 mph	420 mph

It takes car C **8 hours** to catch up with the other cars.

Use Equations

pages 30–32

1. Area of rectangle = 30 × 15

$$= 450 \text{ cm}^2$$

$$20\% \rightarrow \frac{20}{100} \times 450 = 90 \text{ cm}^2 \text{ (shaded)}$$

Area of triangle = $\frac{1}{2} \times 20 \times 30$

$$= 300 \text{ cm}^2$$

Unshaded area = (450 − 90) + (300 − 90)

$$= 570 \text{ cm}^2$$

The area of the unshaded region is **570 square centimeters**.

2. Total area = 6 × 6 + 4 × 4 = 52 cm²

Area of ΔABC = $\frac{1}{2} \times 6 \times 6 = 18 \text{ cm}^2$

Area of ΔCEF = $\frac{1}{2} \times 10 \times 4 = 20 \text{ cm}^2$

52 − 18 − 20 = 14 cm²

The area of the shaded region is **14 square centimeters**.

3.

Sunshine — halfway — Lake; truck→ ←bus

30 mi.   T → $1\frac{1}{4}$ hr.

Distance by bus = 56 × $1\frac{1}{4}$

$$= 70 \text{ mi.}$$

$\frac{1}{2}$ of total distance → 70 + 30

$$= 100 \text{ mi.}$$

Total distance → 100 × 2

$$= 200 \text{ mi.}$$

The distance between the two towns is **200 miles**.

4. Distance traveled by car A = 70 × 6

$$= 420 \text{ mi.}$$

Distance traveled by car B = 780 − 420

$$= 360 \text{ mi.}$$

Speed of car B = 360 ÷ 6

$$= 60 \text{ mph}$$

Car B is traveling at **60 miles per hour**.

Guess and Check

pages 33–35

1.

Adult Ticket	Value	Child Ticket	Value	Total Value	Check
20	$180	20	$120	$300	✗
19	$171	21	$126	$297	✗
18	$162	22	$132	$294	✓

22 child movie tickets were sold.

2.

Motorcycles	Wheels	Cars	Wheels	Trucks	Wheels	Total	Check
20	40	25	100	15	90	230	✗
15	30	30	120	15	90	240	✗
10	20	35	140	15	90	250	✓

10 motorcycles were in the parking lot.

3.

Correct	Points (+)	Incorrect	Points (−)	Total	Check
25	125	25	75	50	✗
30	150	20	60	90	✗
31	155	19	57	98	✓

Ian answered **31 questions** correctly.

4.

$1	Value	$5	Value	$10	Value	Total Value	Check
6	$16	4	$20	3	$30	$56	✗
7	$17	2	$10	4	$40	$57	✗
6	$16	3	$15	4	$40	$61	✓

Libby has **6 $1 bills**, **3 $5 bills**, and **4 $10 bills**.

Before and After
pages 36–38

1. Before: After:

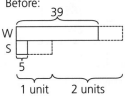

2 units → 39 – 5 = 34

1 unit → 34 ÷ 2 = 17

17 – 5 = 12

Wynona will be 3 times as old as her son in **12 years**.

2. Before: After:

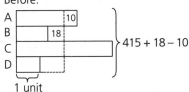

3 units → 350 + 25 = 375

1 unit → 375 ÷ 3 = 125

red → 2 units → 125 × 2 = 250

green → 125 – 25 = 100

Mrs. Taylor bought **250 red apples** and **100 green apples** to begin with.

3. Before: After:

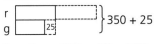

9 units → 415 + 18 – 10 = 423

D → 1 unit → 423 ÷ 9 = 47

C → 4 units → 47 × 4 = 188

2 units → 47 × 2 = 94

B → 94 – 18 = 76

A → 94 + 10 = 104

Tin A had 104 marbles, tin B had 76 marbles, tin C had 188 marbles, and **tin D had 47 marbles** to begin with.

4. Before: After:

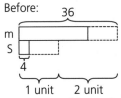

2 units → 36 – 4 = 32

1 unit → 32 ÷ 2 = 16

16 – 4 = 12

Sabena's mother will be 3 times as old as Sabena in **12 years**.

Make Suppositions
pages 39–41

1. Assuming all were child tickets,

40 × $5 = $200

$245 – $200 = $45 (excess)

$8 – $5 = $3

$45 ÷ $3 = 15

The Science Center sold **15 adult tickets**.

2. Assuming all were motorcycles,

55 × 2 = 110

194 – 110 = 84 (excess)

4 – 2 = 2

84 ÷ 2 = 42 cars

55 – 42 = 13 motorcycles

13 motorcycles and **42 cars** were in the parking lot.

3. Assuming Yasmin answered all 40 questions correctly,

40 × 5 = 200

200 – 104 = 96 (shortage)

5 + 3 = 8

96 ÷ 8 = 12 incorrect answers

Yasmin answered **12 questions** incorrectly.

4. Assuming all were blouses,

75 × $12 = $900

$960 – $900 = $60 (excess)

$15 – $12 = $3

$60 ÷ $3 = 20 skirts

75 – 20 = 55 blouses

The store sold **20 skirts** and **55 blouses**.

Mixed Practice: Easy
pages 42–47

1.
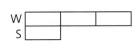

2 units → 40 cm

1 unit → 40 ÷ 2 = 20 cm

8 units → 20 × 8 = 160 cm

The rope was **160 centimeters** long.

2.
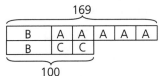

3 units → 169 – 100 = 69

1 unit → 69 ÷ 3 = 23

C → 2 units → 23 × 2 = 46

B → 100 – 46 = 54

54 marbles are in container B.

61

3. Before:

Xander → 10 units

Leo → 21 − 10 = 11 units

21 units → 294

1 unit → 294 ÷ 21 = 14

Xander → 10 units → 14 × 10 = 140

Leo → 11 units → 14 × 11 = 154

After:

Xander → 4 units

Leo → 15 − 4 = 11 units

11 units → 154

1 unit → 154 ÷ 11 = 14

4 units → 14 × 4 = 56

140 − 56 = 84

84 of Xander's mugs were sold.

4. Length = (60 − 10) ÷ 2

$\qquad$ = 25 cm

Breadth = 10 cm

Height = 5 cm

Volume = L × B × H

$\qquad$ = 25 × 10 × 5

$\qquad$ = 1,250 cm³

The volume of the solid is **1,250 cubic centimeters**.

5.

car →
van →

X ←——126 km——→ A

D = 18 km

$T = \frac{3}{8}$ h

Average speed of van = $18 \div \frac{3}{8}$

$\qquad$ = 48 km/h

Time taken by van = 126 ÷ 48

$\qquad$ = 2.625 h

Average speed of car = $126 \div \left(2.625 - \frac{3}{8}\right)$

$\qquad$ = 56 km/h

The **average speed of the car was 56 kilometers per hour**, and the **average speed of the van was 48 kilometers per hour**.

6. lilies → 60% of remaining → 48

daisies → 40% of remaining → $\frac{40}{60} \times 48 = 32$

40% of total → 48 + 32 = 80

100% of total → $\frac{100}{40} \times 80 = 200$

Mr. Garcia ordered **200 flowers**.

7. Each quarter of square ABCD is equivalent to 4 identical small squares.

4 × 4 = 16

The area of square ABCD is **16 square centimeters**.

8.

$1	Value	$5	Value	Total Value	Check
15	$15	10	$50	$65	✗
20	$20	5	$25	$45	✗
21	$21	4	$20	$41	✓

This problem can also be solved by making suppositions.

Assuming all were $1 bills,

25 × $1 = $25

$41 − $25 = $16 (excess)

$5 − $1 = $4

$16 ÷ $4 = 4 pieces of $5 notes

25 − 4 = 21 pieces of $1 notes

Nathan saved **21 $1 bills**.

9. Time taken to walk to school = 480 ÷ 48 = 10 min.

Time taken to walk back from school = 480 ÷ 40 = 12 min.

Total time taken for the round-trip = 10 + 12 = 22 min.

Total distance walked = 480 × 2 = 960 m

Average speed for the round-trip = 960 ÷ 22

$\qquad = 43\frac{7}{11}$ meters

Edgar's average walking speed was **$43\frac{7}{11}$ meters per minute**.

10. Assuming Trey gave all correct answers,

50 × 5 = 250

250 − 152 = 98 (shortage)

5 + 2 = 7

98 ÷ 7 = 14 incorrect answers

50 − 14 = 36 correct answers

Trey answered **36 questions correctly**.

Mixed Practice: Intermediate pages 48–52

1.

36 + 12 = 48

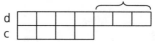

3 units → 48

1 unit → 48 ÷ 3 = 16

4 units → 16 × 4 = 64

In the end, chickens → 64 + 16 = 80

$\qquad$ ducks → 64 + 48 − 12 + 20 = 120

80 + 120 = 200

$\frac{120}{200} \times 100\% = 60\%$

60% of the total number of animals were ducks in the end.

2.

Figure	Number of Dots	Pattern
1	2	1 × 2
2	6	2 × 3
3	12	3 × 4
4	20	4 × 5
34	1,190	34 × 35

1,190 dots will be in Figure 34.

3.

4. Area of quarter circle $= \frac{1}{4} \times \frac{22}{7} \times 7 \times 7$

$$= 38\frac{1}{2} \text{ cm}^2$$

Area of triangle $= \frac{1}{2} \times 7 \times 7$

$$= 24\frac{1}{2} \text{ cm}^2$$

Area of shaded part $= 38\frac{1}{2} - 24\frac{1}{2} = 14 \text{ cm}^2$

The area of the shaded part is **14 square centimeters**.

5.

bus →
left at 1 P.M.   overtook

X ├——————┼————┤ Y

left at 2 P.M. 3 P.M.   3:30 P.M.

car →

Part A   Part B

Part A: car → 1 hour

       bus → 2 hours

This means the speed of the bus is $\frac{1}{2}$ the speed of the car.

Part B: car → $\frac{1}{2}$ hour

       bus → $\frac{1}{2} \times 2 = 1$ hour

The bus reached town Y at **4:00 P.M.**

6. Assuming all were notebooks,

60 × $6 = $360

$384 − $360 = $24 (excess)

$8 − $6 = $2

$24 ÷ $2 = 12 files

60 − 12 = 48 notebooks

Amanda bought **48 notebooks**.

7. 1, 2 → 2 × 1

2, 4 → 2 × 2

3, 6 → 2 × 3

n, $2n$

$\textbf{\textit{t} = 2\textit{n}}$.

8. A + B = 74

B + C = 73

A + C = 71

Adding all, 2A + 2B + 2C = 74 + 73 + 71

                      = 218

A + B + C = 218 ÷ 2 = 109

        C = 109 − 74 = 35

        B = 109 − 71 = 38

        A = 109 − 73 = 36

36 students are in class A, 38 students are in class B, and **35 students are in class C.**

9.

	Caron	Danielle
End	21	29
Caron gave $\frac{2}{5}$ to Danielle	3 units → 21 1 unit → 7 5 units → 35	29 − 7 × 2 = 15
Danielle gave $\frac{1}{2}$ to Caron	35 − 15 = 20	15 × 2 = 30
Caron gave $\frac{1}{3}$ to Danielle	2 units → 20 1 unit → 10 3 units → 30	30 − 10 = 20

Caron had 30 beads and **Danielle had 20 beads** to begin with.

10. Before: After:

4 units → 270 + 18 = 288

1 unit → 288 ÷ 4 = 72

cupcakes → 3 units → 72 × 3 = 216

muffins → 72 − 18 = 54

Mr. Zucco baked **216 cupcakes** and **54 muffins** to begin with.

Mixed Practice: Challenging   pages 53–56

1. The last digits are in the following pattern:

3, 9, 7, 1, 3, 9, . . .

⎵ groups of 4

99 ÷ 4 = 24 R 3

3rd position → 7

The last digit of 3^{99} is **7**.

2.

Jack	Jaelynn
10	30
10 × 2 = 20	30 − 10 = 20
20 − 20 = 0	20 × 2 = 40
0 + 8 = 8	40 − 8 = 32

Jack had 8 trading cards and **Jaelynn had 32 trading cards** to begin with.

3. $30 × 2 = $60
$60 + $50 = $110
$110 × 2 = $220
$220 + $100 = $320
$320 × 2 = $640
Ken brought **$640** on his trip.

4.

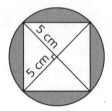

Area of circle
= 3.14 × 5 × 5
= 78.5 cm²
Area of square
= 4 × $\frac{1}{2}$ × 5 × 5
= 50 cm²
Area of shaded region = 78.5 − 50 = 28.5 cm²
The area of the shaded region is **28.5 square centimeters**.

5. Before:

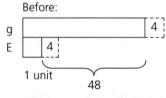

After:

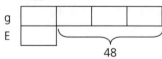

3 units → 48
1 unit → 48 ÷ 3 = 16
4 units → 16 × 4 = 64
64 − 4 = 60
Erica's grandmother is **60 years old**.

6. Assuming all the pizzas were delivered on time,
15 × $20 = $300
$300 − $291 = $9 (shortage)
100% − 15% = 85%
$\frac{85}{100}$ × $20 = $17
$20 − $17 = $3
$9 ÷ $3 = 3 (late)
15 − 3 = 12 (on time)
The pizza shop delivered **12 pizzas** on time.

7.

Number of square faces = 6
Number of triangular faces = 8
6 + 8 = 14
The solid has **14 faces**.
It is called a cuboctahedron.

8. Divide the square into 4 triangles.

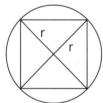

The base of each small triangle is the radius of the circle.

Area of each small triangle = 72 ÷ 4
= 18 cm²
So $\frac{1}{2}$ × r × r = 18 cm²
r × r = 36 cm²
r = 6 cm
Area of circle = πr²
= $\frac{22}{7}$ × 6 × 6
= $113\frac{1}{7}$ cm²

The area of the circle is **$113\frac{1}{7}$ square centimeters**.